£6.99

WELCOME TO THE BEANO ANNUAL 2006

© D. C. Thomson & Co., Ltd. Printed and published by D. C. Thomson & Co., Ltd., 185 Fleet Street, London EC4A 2HS. ISBN 1 84535 042 1

PHTRYP!

TIME TO GET RID OF THIS BABY MUSH THROUGH MY TOOTH GAP.

And –

SPLUTCH!

CAN'T SEE! I'VE BEEN MUSHED!

OO! THAT MUST HAVE HURT!

IT DID!

CRUMP!

BEA CAN STAND IN FOR HIM - SHE'S THE BEST DRIBBLER IN THE BEANO!

EEK! SHE'S DRIBBLING FROM HER NAPPY!

WE COULD HAVE BOBBY MOORE.

HOW ARE YOU GOING TO DO HIM?

Dribbling again!

I'LL HEAD OUT OF TOWN TO ANOTHER SORT OF MOOR...

ZOOM!

...BEANOTOWN MOOR - I'LL NEED THIS TURF...

BEANOTOWN MOOR

Back home-

...TO MAKE MY BOBBY MOORE STATUE. COOL, EH?

FREDDIE FEAR

...the werewolf cubs were all full up, humans never set foot in that part of Transylvania again, and they all lived happily ever after – the end! Wasn't that a good bedtime story, Fred?

Er... maybe not! Maybe I could make you some hot milk to help you sleep, Fred...

No need – I'll do it myself! I'm wide-awake, thanks to your spooky bedtime stories!!

Huh! Maybe I SHOULD'VE let Mum make me hot milk, after all! Look out for more spooky stories throughout the book, readers!

DEREK the SHEEP in "ONE FOR THE POT!"

Aah! This is the life!

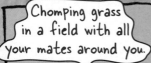

Chomping grass in a field with all your mates around you.

And only the gentle buzz of a bee or rustle of leaves to disturb you!

What fool wouldn't want to be a sheep, eh?

OW!!

sting!

bzzz

Move your bum, fatso!

Blummin' cheek!

Whatever.

Bees — I hate 'em!

NO-O-O!

THUMP THWUUP!

BILLY THE CAT! HOW DID YOU ESCAPE?

NOT THAT I'M COMPLAINING...

CATS HAVE CLAWS... REMEMBER?

YOU... YOU HAVE YOUR OWN GLASS CUTTER?

THE MULLIGAN MOB... THEY'RE GETTING AWAY!

OH, I DON'T THINK THAT'S GOING TO HAPPEN SOMEHOW.

L S LOWRY

THE DANDY ARTIST

MANGA

JRR TOLKEIN

EGYPTIAN HIEROGLYPHICS

DANNY and SPOTTY in "SHUT YOUR TRAP!"

SPOTTY TRIES AGAIN LATER IN THIS BOOK

LiTTLE PLUM

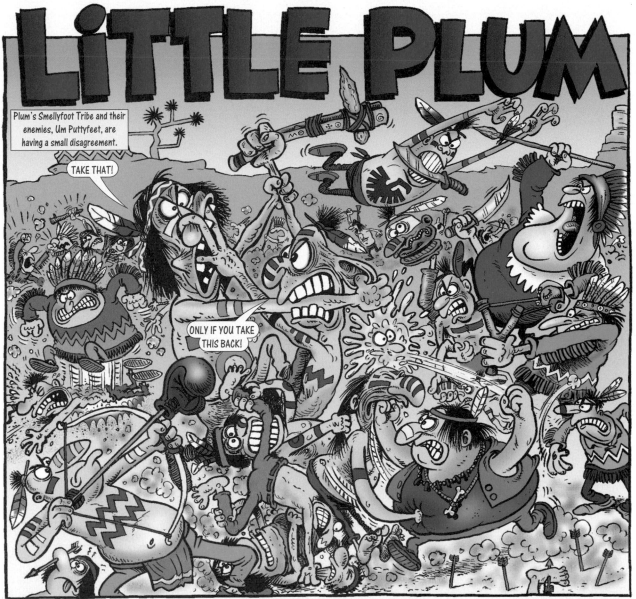

PLUM 083a

BE A SPORT

LES PRETEND

Presently —

So —

THE BASH STREET KIDS IN...

WE'RE LATE!

VERY LATE!

IN FACT, WE'RE...

...HOLY BALONY!

AHOY THERE, SHIPMATES!

A LOAD OF JUNK!

SCRUNCH! SCRUNCH! SCRUNCH!

I'VE HEARD OF SCHOOL SUBS, BUT THIS IS RIDICULOUS!

MIKE PEARSE

MEANWHILE...

KNOCK! KNOCK!

COME IN...!

HEAD MASTER

HEADMASTER, AN ENORMOUS MESS HAS BEEN MADE IN THIS SCHOOL!

THAT'S DISGRACEFUL!

WELCOME

GROVEL

A DOOR HAS BEEN RIPPED OFF ITS HINGES...!

TERRIBLE! SHOCKING!

... AND BOOKS COVER THE FLOOR!

OUTRAGEOUS! UNACCEPTABLE!

WELL, DON'T WORRY ABOUT A THING!

THANK YOU...

I'LL GET THE CARETAKER TO CLEAN IT UP.

THE BEANO

THAT WAS TIME WELL SPENT!

HEAD MASTER

④

AND SO...

GRUMBLE! GRUMBLE!

SCRUNCH! SCRUNCH!

ALL RIGHT, CLASS, NOW I'VE SHOWN YOU HOW IT'S DONE...

...I WANT YOU TO MAKE YOUR OWN WORKS OF ART USING OBJECTS YOU FIND AROUND THE SCHOOL...!

RIGHT! COME ON!

LET'S GO!

URK!

MY WORD! I'VE NEVER SEEN THE KIDS SHOW THAT MUCH ENTHUSIASM!

REALLY...

PERHAPS I'VE FINALLY TAPPED INTO THEIR ARTISTIC SPIRIT!

THIS IS GREAT!

YEAH!

WE GET TO MAKE A MESS *WITH TEACHER'S PERMISSION!*

POC!

⑤

MEANWHILE ...

RIGHT! I THINK I'VE GIVEN THOSE KIDS ENOUGH TIME ...

...LET'S SEE WHAT THEY'RE UP TO!

IN THE SCHOOL KITCHEN ...

HELLO, TEACH!

WE'RE MAKING SCULPTURES FROM LEFTOVER FOOD!

WHAT A MARVELLOUS IDEA!

ISN'T IT? ... SLURP!

AND ON THE PLAYGROUND ...

HOW'S THE WORK OF ART COMING ALONG?

COULDN'T BE BETTER!

GREAT! NOW WHERE ARE TOOTS AND SIDNEY?

CLONK!

7

WHERE INDEED..?

KNOCK! KNOCK!

NOW WHAT?!

HEAD MASTER

THESE TWO CHILDREN HAVE MADE A MESS OF MY TABLECLOTH!

DISGRACEFUL! WHAT DO YOU BOTH HAVE TO SAY FOR YOURSELVES?!

WE'RE KIDS! OF COURSE WE MADE A MESS ON THE TABLECLOTH!

WHAT KID DOESN'T?

BESIDES, WHY CAN'T OLIVE JUST WASH IT?

I DID WASH IT, YOUNG LADY!

SO WHAT ARE WE DOING HERE THEN?

NO ... BUT YOU SEE... ...WHAT HAPPENED WAS ... ER ...

DRUM! DRUM!

ALL RIGHT, YOU MAY HAVE GOT AWAY WITH IT THIS TIME ...!

...BUT I'VE GOT MY EYE ON YOU!

HEAD MASTER

8

MEANWHILE, ON THE PLAYGROUND...

...BUT, SPOTTY, WHAT *IS* IT?

THAT DEPENDS HOW YOU LOOK AT IT, DANNY...

GRUMBLE! GRUMBLE!

...TO ME, IT'S AN ALIEN ROBOT!

NAH..!

...IT'S A MUTANT DINOSAUR!

YOU'RE BOTH WRONG! IT'S A GIANT FLEA!

WAIT! LET'S GET AN OUTSIDE OPINION...!

WHAT DO *YOU* THINK IT IS?

WHAT A HIDEOUS MESS!

AND YET ANOTHER INTERPRETATION!

GRRRR...!

I DON'T THINK HE'S A FAN OF MODERN ART!

9

11

...IT'S A MASTER-PIECE!

MY WORD! THAT'S ARCHIBALD FANSHAW!

WHO?!?

HE'S A FAMOUS ART COLLECTOR!

...WHO HAPPENS TO WANDER INTO THE GIRLS' CHANGING ROOMS OF A LOCAL SCHOOL?!

WHO WRITES THIS RUBBISH?!

SCRIPT

WHY, THIS YOUNG MAN IS A GENIUS!

A GENIUS..?

SMIFFY..?

HA! HA! HA! HA! HA! HA! HA! HA! HA! HA! HA! HA! HA! HA!

WILL A CHEQUE FOR TEN THOUSAND POUNDS BE ENOUGH?

ER ... I SUPPOSE...

HA! HA! HA! HA! HA! HA! HA! HA! HA!

10,000

THANKS...

HA...HA...HA.. ...HA...HA...HA. ..AA..AAAA...

£

So-

FREDDIE'S DEATH-BEDTIME STORIES

Aaaaah! Lovely, comfy bed!

Mmmmmm! Lovely porridge!

Magic – I do love to sit in my comfy chair to watch television!

YIKES!

Who's been eating MYYYYYY porridge???

N-n-n-not u-u-u-us!

This is one of Mum's fave bedtime stories – GHOULdilocks And The Three Bears!!!

DAVE EASTBURY

...TO MAKE A DELIGHTFUL SNOWFLAKE DESIGN...

...UNFORTUNATELY HER POOR FATHER WAS DOING A SPONSORED PARARACHUTE JUMP THAT DAY...

IVY HAD GONE TOO FAR AS USUAL!

WHOOOSH!

ME DID THAT! GOOD DESIGN, EH?

GVORP!

LUCKILY THE PIG FARM BROKE HIS FALL.

RIP!

BUT IVY USED THE NEW WALLPAPER IN HER BATHROOM...

...AND BRITNEY AND KYLIE NEEDED COUNSELLING AFTER IVY WENT TOO FAR AS USUAL.

I MADE A POTATO HEDGEHOG OUT OF A HALF POTATO STUFFED WITH DAMP COTTON-WOOL AND GRASS SEED.

JAG!

YEOWL!

IVY WENT TOO FAR USING A TURNIP AND THISTLES!

DAVE EASTBURY

LITTLE PLUM

WELL, HELLO-O-O-O!

I'M OUTTA HERE!

OH, NO! IT'S UM RATHER TOO ENTHUSIASTIC DANCE TEACHER.

ME TOO!

RIGHT, PLUM DEARIE. LET ME SEE UM RAIN DANCE MOVES I SHOWED YOU.

Plum struts his stuff...

SHUFFLE SHUFFLE

SPROING

TWIRL TWIDDLE

PLUM 089-A

And-

OW! OO! YOWL!
NOT RIGHT! NOT RIGHT!

Plum tries again-

WHAT UM MOVER, EH?

Alas-

NO! NO! WRONG DANCE AGAIN!

PANT PANT

And-

BONG!
YEOWCH!

HUNT EMERSON

I WALKED INTO UM TOTEM-POLE COS I COULDN'T SEE.

AW! SHAME!

ONCE MORE, FOLKS!

MAKE YOUR VERY OWN

Start by making up the head and neck then make the body.

Materials you will need —
● A pencil and scissors.
● A sheet of A4 white paper and a piece of medium thickness white card.
● An empty toilet roll tube.
● Sticky tape and a glue stick.
● Two pipecleaners (craft shops sell these)
● Black paint (water mixable).
● Cotton wool.

To make the head and neck.

Start by tracing the shapes on to paper that you can see the design through, or, if you can, photocopy the page, then, glue the design on to medium thickness card. Cut out round the solid black lines and fold along the dotted lines, then glue together as instructions.

2 EYES AND EARS

APPLY GLUE TO THIS SIDE THEN STICK TO TOP OF HEAD **A** WHEN GLUE HAS SET FOLD UP EYES AND EARS

1 HEAD

FOLD DOWN AND GLUE TO UNDERSIDE OF HEAD

D | C

B

FOLD DOWN

FOLD DOWN

GLUE EYES AND EARS HERE

A

GLUE TO UNDERSIDE

GLUE TO UNDERSIDE

FOLD DOWN

3 NECK

GLUE THESE TWO TABS ONTO BODY

FOLD UP

FOLD UP

FOLD DOWN AND GLUE TO THE INSIDE OF NECK

D | C

FOLD UP THESE TWO TABS GLUE TO THE UNDERSIDE OF HEAD **B**

✳ LINE UP ARROW ON NECK WITH ARROW ON UNDER SIDE OF HEAD **B**

First make up the head, then glue the eyes and ears to the top of the head A. Then make up the neck and glue it to the inside of the head B. The head is now ready to glue to the body.

DEREK the SHEEP

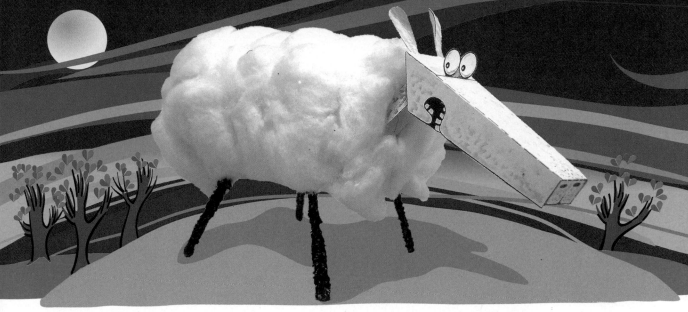

To make the body and legs.

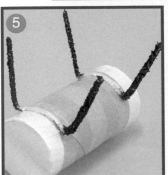

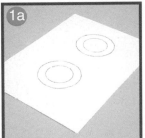

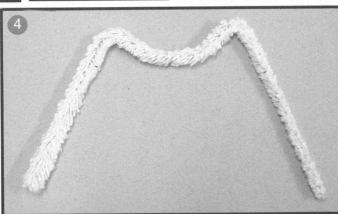

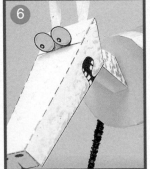

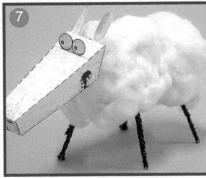

1. Take the toilet roll tube and place it end down on the piece of paper, draw round it to get the circle size, then repeat this process for the second circle, now draw another circle about 15 mm round the outside of the circles already drawn, illustration 1a.

2. Cut out the two circles and snip up to the inner circle at about 20 mm intervals all the way round, then bend the tabs down.

3. Glue or tape the two cut out circles on to each end of the tube.

4. Take the two pipecleaners and bend them to the shape on the page, illustration 4.

5. Firmly tape the legs to the tube about 20cm from both ends. You can now paint the legs black.

6. Now you can glue the head and neck (a bit higher than the centre) on to one end of the tube.

7. All that is left to do now is to glue on the cotton wool and 'Derek' is complete.

GENERAL JUMBO
JUMBO JOHNSON OWNS AN AMAZING MINIATURE ARMY MADE FOR HIM BY HIS FRIEND, PROFESSOR CARTER. JUMBO IS ON HOLIDAY AT BEACON COTTAGE IN THE PRETTY SEASIDE VILLAGE OF BRINEHARBOUR.
Keith Robson '04

BE A SPORT

HAR-HAR! I'M PREPARING THE BALLS FOR THE BASH STREET TEACHER'S TENNIS TOURNAMENT.

COOEE! I'M HOME WITH THE SHOPPING. HAD A LITTLE BUMP IN THE CAR, BUT NEVER MIND!

THESE SOFTY BALLOONISTS ARE GONNA GET A SHARP REMINDER OF MY MENACING SKILL.

LET'S BE LIKE THOSE GUYS BEHIND US - LET'S CUDDLE!

FREDDIE FEAR

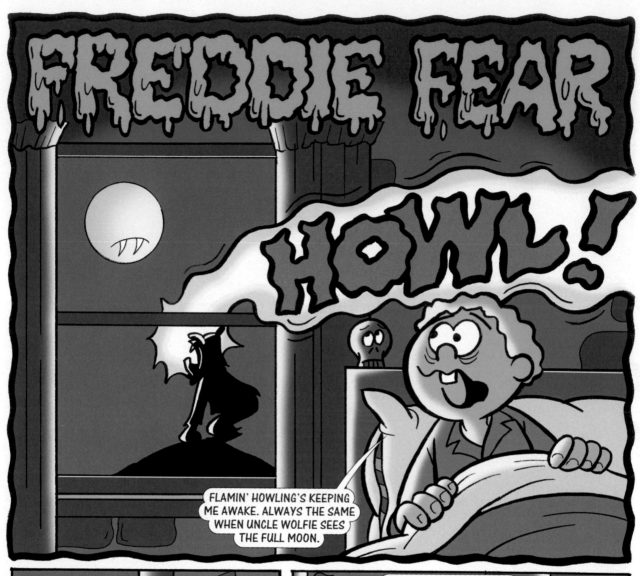

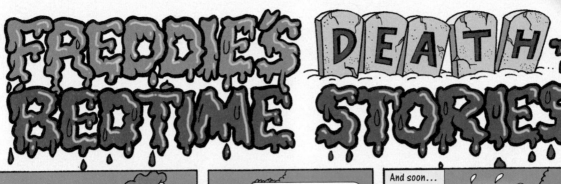

FREDDIE'S DEATH-BEDTIME STORIES

DAVE EASTBURY

LOOK – PRIVATE FOO-FOO. LOOKS LIKE HE'S GOT A MISSION FOR THE S.A.S.

ZOOM!

YIP – YAP – YIPPITY YAPPITY YOPPITY – YUPPITTY.

OH, MY GIDDY AUNT! BRACE YOURSELVES, CHUMMIES!

TREMBLE

DOGGY DICTIONARY

SO, SPRAY ME WITH PERFUME, WOULD YOU?

BUT, YOU SMELL SO – WELL – ER – STINKY!

BOUNCE

BOING!

WE'RE TOO LATE.

BOING!

TICKLE!

MRS SNODGRASS

MY POOR, WOUNDED, LITTLE SOLDIER.

… HIS MUMMY!

CHUCKLE!

THERE, THERE! DON'T WORRY, LITTLE LAMB. I'LL SOON …

… KISS IT BETTER! THERE!

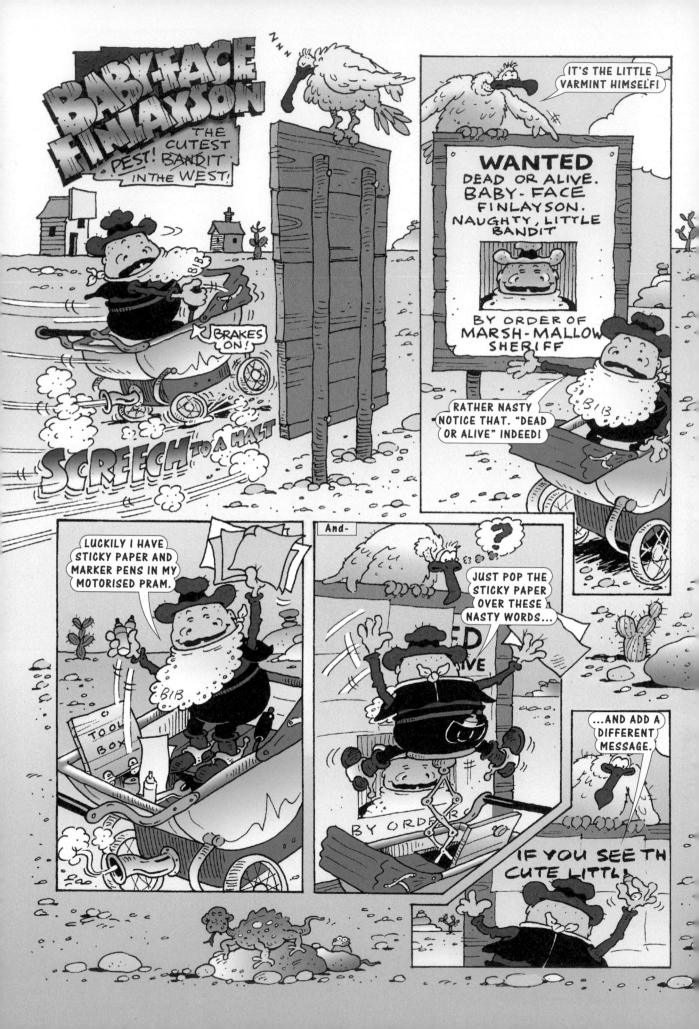

HEAD FOR PLANET BEANO —

THE STAR COMIC IN THE UNIVERSE!

BEANO